Investigate

Rocks and Soil

Charlotte Guillain

Heinemann Library
Chicago, Illinois

2008 Heinemann Library
a division of Pearson Inc.
Chicago, Illinois

Customer Service 888-454-2279
Visit our website at www.heinemannraintree.com

Designed by Joanna Hinton-Malivoire Victoria Bevan, and Hart McLeod
Printed in China by Leo Paper Group

12 11 10 09 08
10 9 8 7 6 5 4 3 2 1

The Library of Congress has cataloged the first edition as follows:
Guillain, Charlotte.
  Rocks and soil / Charlotte Guillain. -- 1st ed.
      p. cm. -- (Investigate)
  Includes bibliographical references and index.
  ISBN 978-1-4329-1395-3 (hc) -- ISBN 978-1-4329-1411-0 (pb) 1. Rocks--Juvenile literature. 2. Soils--Juvenile literature. I. Title.
  QE432.2.G85 2008
  552--dc22
                              2008007262

Acknowledgments
The publishers would like to thank the following for permission to reproduce photographs: ©Alamy pp. **4** (Liz Boyd), **5** (Patrick Eden), **15** (Frances Roberts), **20** (David Hoffman Photo Library), **21** (Crops galore/Den Reader), **28** (Chris Howes/Wild Places Photography); ©Brand X Pictures p. **13** (Photo 24. 2001); ©Corbis pp. **7**, **10**, **22**; ©DK Images p. **16**; ©FLPA p. **27** (Mitsuaki Iwago/Minden Pictures); ©Getty Images p. **8** (Digital Vision), **11** (Bob Stefko), **12** (Darrell Gulin), **14** (James Worrell), **17** (Lars Borges), **23** (Darrin Klimek), **29** (Steven Wooster); ©PhotoDisc p. **7** (Siede Pries); ©Photolibrary p. **6** (Corbis), **18** (Magnus Hjorleifsson), **26** (David M. Dennis); ©Rex Features p. **25** (E. M. Welch); ©Science Photo Library p. **9** (Michael Szoenyi), **19** (David Nunuk), **24** (David C. Clegg).

Cover photograph reproduced with permission of ©NaturePL (David Welling).

Contents

Some words are shown in bold, **like this**. You can find out what they mean by looking in the glossary.

What Are Rocks and Soil?

Rocks and soil are all around us. Rocks and soil are **nonliving**. They come from Earth.

Soil is the top layer of Earth's surface. Rocks are found underneath the soil. Rocks are also found underneath water.

Rocks

There is a thick layer of rock all over Earth's surface. You can see rocks at the beach or by rivers.

⬆ You can see rocks in the mountains.

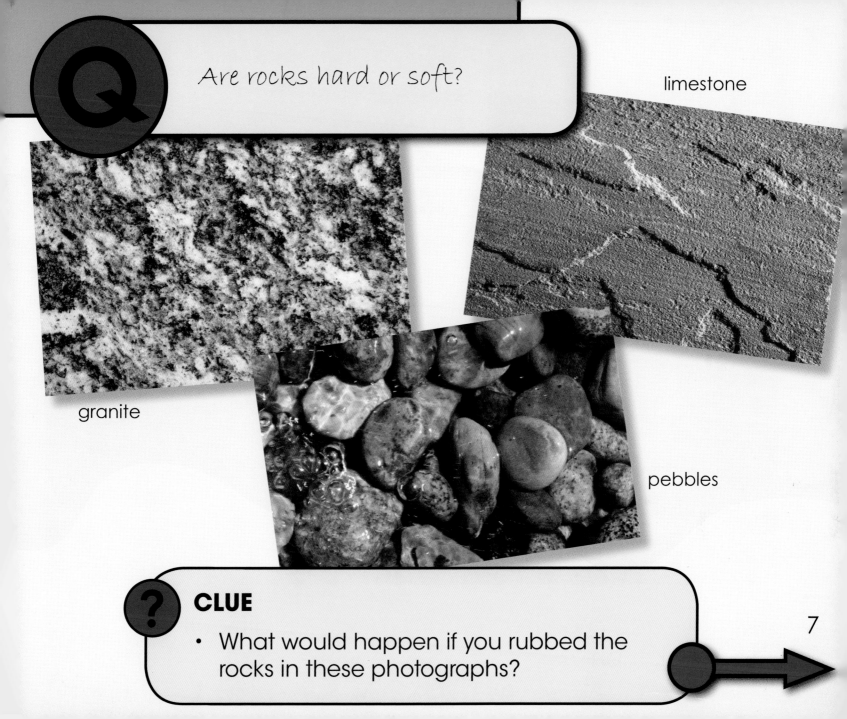

Are rocks hard or soft?

limestone

granite

pebbles

CLUE

- What would happen if you rubbed the rocks in these photographs?

7

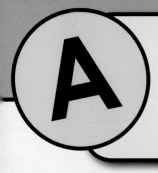

Some rocks are very hard. They do not change if you rub them. Some rocks are softer. They break into pieces if you rub them.

8   Marble and granite are hard rocks. It is difficult to break them.

Rocks are made up of different **minerals**. Minerals change how a rock looks and feels. Rocks with the mineral iron in them are hard.

9

Chalk and sandstone are softer rocks. They wear away if you rub them.

→ Chalk is soft and rubs off, which means you can write with it.

Water, wind, and the Sun's heat wear down all types of rock. The rocks break into small pieces. This is called **erosion**.

Q Where could you see rocks that have been broken down?

? CLUE
• Where do you find a lot of water?

A You can see rocks that have been broken down at the beach or by a river.

At the seashore, the waves move against the rock and slowly wear it away.

12

Rivers and streams slowly wear away rock as they flow. The small pieces of rock are carried in the river and wear away more of the **riverbed**. After many years, this **erosion** can form **valleys**.

valley

valley

Ways We Use Rocks

We use different rocks in different ways. We can use hard rocks for building. Other hard rocks, such as diamonds, can be used to make jewelry.

We use soft rocks, such as chalk and graphite, to draw and write.

 Graphite is used in pencils.

15

Soil

Soil is made up of tiny pieces of rock that have broken up. It is also made of pieces of plants, such as leaves and twigs. There are even tiny parts of animals that lived long ago mixed into soil.

Soils can be different colors and **textures**. This dark soil is called peat.

Q What type of soil do you find near the ocean?

CLUE
- What covers a beach?

17

**A**

The soil near the ocean is usually made of sand. Sand is mainly made of broken down rocks and shells.

 ←

Beaches are made up of sand and pieces of rock.

Silt is a very fine soil. It has a lot of water and food for plants in it. Silt is a good soil for growing plants.

Chalky soil has a lot of stones in it and dries out very quickly. It does not hold much water or food for plants. Chalk is not a good soil for growing plants.

Some soils, such as clay, do not dry out quickly.
Puddles of water will stay for a long time in clay
soil. Peat is another soil with a lot of water in it.

Ways We Use Soil

We use soil to grow plants for food. These plants include wheat, rice, vegetables, and fruit.

Q What type of soil do we use to make pots?

We can also use soil to make things.

CLUE

• It is easy to shape with your hands.

A

We can use clay to make pots. Clay soil is brown, red, or gray. The rocks that broke down to make the soil were also brown, red, or gray.

24

We can also use clay to build houses. Another soil we can use to build with is sand. We use sand to make cement, which is also used for building.

Many animals use soil. Some animals, such as earthworms, live in soil. Earthworms eat the small pieces of plants and animals in the soil.

Earthworms' tunnels help get plenty of air and water into the soil.

termite mound

Some animals use soil to build their homes. Swallows make their nests with mud. Termites make their **mounds** out of soil.

27

Rocks and soils can be many different colors, shapes, and sizes. Some rocks are hard, and some rocks are soft.

Soil is mostly broken down rock. Soil and rocks are **natural resources**. People and animals use rocks and soils in many different ways to help them live.

29

Checklist

➠ Rocks and soil are **nonliving**.

➠ Rocks and soil are **natural resources**.

➠ Rocks are made of **minerals**. They can be hard or soft.

➠ All rock is broken down by **erosion**.

➠ Soil is made of tiny pieces of rock, plants, and animals that lived long ago.

Some soils are made of large pieces, and some are made of very small, fine pieces. This is because soils are made from different types of rock.

Glossary

chalky soft, fine, white type of soil

erosion wearing away of land by sun, wind, or water

mineral nonliving material from Earth

mound pile or heap

natural resource material from Earth that we can use

nonliving not alive

riverbed soil and rocks at the bottom of a river

silt fine type of soil that is good for growing plants

texture how something feels

valley dip in the land between hills

Index